To Mattie Floyd

The Trials of Life
Will not Destroy The
Heart of Faith!

Stay Encouraged

This Is MY SPOT!

-Celebrating My Position in Christ-

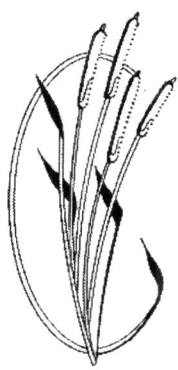

This Is MY SPOT!

-Celebrating My Position in Christ-

by Pastor Jake Gaines, Jr.

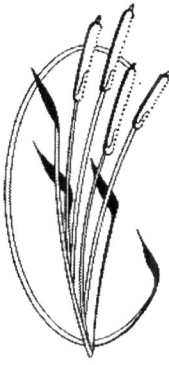

Editor
Ray Glandon

Cover Design
Leona Gaines

Photography & Graphics
*C C Photography Enterprise
LLC*

Senior Publisher
Steven Hill

Awarded Publishing House
ASA Publishing Company

A Publisher Trademark Title page

ASA Publishing Corporation
An Accredited Publishing House with the BBB

105 E. Front St., Suite 101
Monroe, Michigan 48161
www.asapublishingcorporation.com

Copyrights©2015 Pastor Jake Gaines, Jr., All Rights Reserved
Book: This Is MY SPOT *Celebrating My Position in Christ*
Date Published: 04.06.14/Edition 1 *Trade Paperback*
Book ASAPCID: 2380671
ISBN: 978-1-886528-94-9
Library of Congress Cataloging-in-Publication Data

This book was published in the United States of America.
State of Michigan

A Publisher Trademark Copy page

Table of Contents

Words of Encouragement

Dr. Clifford Register

President of William/Moss/Copeland/King-Parker, Baptist Seminary (W.M.C.K.-Parker), Detroit, Michigan

It was not by chance, but by God's divine choosing that our lives intersected. My once limited knowledge of God has been enhanced down through the years by your mentoring and friendship. Such life changing experiences have helped me become the preacher I am today. I, as well as many others, have benefited from your teaching, preaching and writings. It is a reflection of your labor of love. I pray that you will continue to exercise the spiritual gifts with which GOD has blessed you, to help others develop the spiritual fortitude necessary to transcend the obstacles and challenges of life. *"Fight the good fight of faith, lay hold on eternal life, whereunto thou art also called, and hast professed a good profession before many witnesses".* (I Timothy 6:12)

Your Friend and Brother in Christ

Words of Encouragement

Rev. Danny Sanders

My Son in Ministry
Atlanta, Georgia

Pastor, I encourage you to continue to allow God to use you in such an awesome way. You are such a blessing to me and my ministry. We truly need more ambassadors of Christ who are committed to sharing the Word of God. I am truly proud of you. Thank you for being my **"Spiritual Father."** God has given you wisdom and knowledge to reach the hearts of the broken, fragmented, and forlorn, to provide hope for their lives and eternity.

When I am in bookstores and see people picking up your books and browsing through them, I stick my chest out and say to myself, that's **"My Daddy."** (LOL)

Love You Pastor,

Danny

Introduction

When you genuinely receive Christ as "Lord and Savior," it entails more than just becoming a member of a church. Something phenomenal occurs *immediately*. It's not something you can see with the naked eye, yet it's as powerful, influential and divine as everlasting life itself.

Upon your genuine commitment to follow Christ, your destiny changes drastically. The foundation of your life takes on a new and exciting meaning.

"Salvation," which is deliverance or rescue from the condemnation of sin through the blood of Jesus Christ, may be quite new to you at this point, and you may have little knowledge of the intricacies involved in its great work. However, experiencing it immediately changes your "position" in life. Provided you are truly sincere in your profession to receive Christ as your Lord and Savior, you will have a new and immediate position by which you are highly favored.

You immediately move from:

- ✟ Sinner to saint
- ✟ Lost to found
- ✟ Condemned to redeemed
- ✟ Fragmented to whole
- ✟ Darkness to light
- ✟ Guilty to acquitted

Though your immediate circumstances do not change, many wonderful things occur instantly that do not immediately impact your everyday life experiences yet are valuable to your existence.

All of this, and more, occurs in the twinkling of an eye. You have now become a "child of God," as opposed to just being "his creation." You are no longer an enemy of God. You have immediately obtained a new position that entitles you to intimacy with God.

Romans 5:10 (TLB) And since, when we were his enemies, we were brought back to God by the death of his Son, what blessings he must have for us now that we are his friends and he is living within us!

Through his grace you are no longer estranged from God as a result of sin. All of your sins (transgressions against God) have been forgiven, and you have **"new life,"** thus a new position that I like to call, **MY SPOT.**

Understanding this position and its value will help you fight against the trickery of Satan, who desires to mentally and emotionally dislodge you from this new position through the ups, downs and nuances of life. He will use any tactics available to him in order to accomplish this objective. Therefore, beware!

It's supremely important that we understand the significance of this position as a child of God. I am currently in my 29th year of serving as Pastor of Synagogue Baptist Church, and I thank God for the privilege. It saddens me, however, that during that span of time I have noticed a pattern among many congregants that continues to burden me. It is their lack of understanding and/or their unwillingness to claim their position in Christ.

What does it really mean to be a child of God in our everyday experience? Being a child of God means we have been cleansed by the blood that Jesus shed upon the cross. Now we can have an intimate relationship with God. Without Jesus paying the price for our transgressions, this blessed position could never have been awarded us because prior to accepting Jesus Christ as our Messiah we were permanently separated from God. However, if you have accepted him, yet do not understand the position you now find yourself, the efforts of the Holy Spirit to mold you into the Christ-like image you desire could be circumvented, and this will have a negative effect on your everyday experiences.

This new position means that you have been made right with God, you have been reconciled to God the Father in terms of your relationship, and that determines how God responds to you. You are now pleasing to him, and you have his favor ... not because of your performance but because of your position.

I am firmly convinced that it is the lack of understanding this position that causes many of God's children to become lackadaisical, if not downright careless in their spiritual growth. This often results in them being constantly discouraged in their Christian journey.

Your position as a child of God immediately affords you divine purpose in life because God has a unique plan for you as his child. You gain immediate credibility and value based on **"whose"** you are as opposed to "*who*" you are.

It is this personal relationship with God that will set you apart from your environment. Your value is no longer determined based upon your current circumstances. It will never be about where you are. It is where you are headed in the will of God.

This is not only liberating for me but also extremely encouraging to know that my circumstances can never hold me hostage and keep me from the plan that God has ordained. You must never lose sight of your new position in Christ. The less we know about our position in Christ Jesus, the easier it is for Satan to keep us bound in emotional and psychological prisons.

We often do not realize that we're emotionally incarcerated. God wants us to be free from this life sentence of brokenness and futile flailing at life itself. If you have not yet given your life to God through Jesus Christ, I pray that after reading this book you will consider surrendering to his bounty of love and grace.

If you have received Christ as Lord, yet you find your Christian experience to be quite burdensome and unfulfilling, it's imperative that you recognize your uniqueness and value as a human being through the eyes of God. After all these years, I continue to be excited about my position in Christ because he continues to have purpose for my life. That's why I fondly call this positon, "**MY SPOT.**"

Let's get started and see if we can gain a new appreciation for our position in Christ Jesus.

This Is MY SPOT!

-Celebrating My Position in Christ-

by Pastor Jake Gaines, Jr.

Chapter 1

MY SPOT, God's Space

John 15: 4 (TLB) Take care to live in me, and let me live in you. For a branch can't produce fruit when severed from the vine. Nor can you be fruitful apart from me.

Jesus said this directly to his disciples who had accepted him as the Messiah. These words are not directed to those who continued to reject and remain hostile toward God, but to his people. Therefore, it is clear that he is talking to the redeemed that need to understand the value of this unique relationship and the importance of remaining faithful to it. It is all about productivity in the Kingdom of God, despite the challenges we must face.

To be **"in Christ"** is a term that connotes to faithfully be **"with"** him, to remain unified with him. It is to remain faithful to him as a way of life.

It is a divine connection through the power of the Holy Spirit that should be manifested constantly, which allows God to get the glory through our physical existence. It is a cognitive decision, not a roll of the dice, to be identified with Christ as holy and set apart unto God.

To be **"in Christ"** is to not be ashamed to be associated with him and his statutes. It is standing firm on his way of thinking and his methods, no matter how antithetical it may be to mainstream thinking.

Being in Christ, **MY SPOT**, is a place of refuge, restoration, and victory. However, though it's a safe place, it is not a place devoid of responsibility. What is often lost in the frenzy and blessed hope of this new freedom in Christ is the responsibility to mature in our experience, which is solely determined by our level of commitment.

Salvation is free because it is totally based upon God's initiative through his grace (undeserved favor) and not our ability to earn it. (Romans 4:1-5). However, spiritual growth and walking in this newness are not experienced without a sincere and disciplined effort on our part. It requires work and commitment. We often misconstrue the idea that the freedom that we receive in Christ relieves us of our responsibility. This can be fatal to the Christian growth process to those who believe that they are protected by some magical environment of divinity.

Being saved and safe is a new beginning by which we approach life through the eyes of God. However, it is not effortless. It is hard work, but the end results are worth it. The freedom of divine truth and reality unleashes a power that you have never experienced in its entirety. You stop living a life that is based on a *"relative truth,"* which depends, in part, on particular circumstances, ethnicities, customs, and personal viewpoints. In this new position you begin to live your life based on the absolute and unequivocal truth of God that transcends time, space and people.

Though I bask in my new spot that affords me intimacy with God, it is **MY SPOT** only because of the privilege to reside within it. It is still God's space as it pertains to ownership. It's not **MY SPOT** to govern as I choose but a spot that is shrouded with the

"blood of Jesus" and permeated with his love for me, that I might serve him to his glory and not my own. It is a spot in which I can stand boldly for God and live by his standards through his power.

This is one of the primary reasons that the devil wishes us to reside in this spot very nonchalantly, and often carelessly, without the proper demeanor to stand guard appropriately. (1st Peter 5:8) This way he can continue to have a major influence in our thinking, and thus, in our lives. Satan does not want us to be keenly aware of **"whose"** we are but **"who"** we are or are not.

This may not seem to be important at the outset of our journey, but it is crucial as it pertains to our ability to endure through ups and downs. Though who we are in Christ is important, it is not vital that others always understand or approve of us. Whether others see you **"as all you can be"** is not of extreme importance. God will judge us. We often give too much value to the opinions of others as we labor for their acceptance at every turn. We want everyone to show us approval, love and admiration. This is the opposite of what Christ told his disciples.

A S A   P u b l i s h i n g   C o r p o r a t i o n

John 15: 16-19 (TLB) [16] "You didn't choose me! I chose you! I appointed you to go and produce lovely fruit always, so that no matter what you ask for from the Father, using my name, he will give it to you. [17] I demand that you love each other, [18] for you get enough hate from the world! But then, it hated me before it hated you. [19] The world would love you if you belonged to it; but you don't—for I chose you to come out of the world, and so it hates you.

One of the most effective devices that Satan employs is to convince us to take the principles and ideals of society and attempt to incorporate them into the Kingdom of God. This will always result in an effort in futility. No matter how hard we try to mix them, **IT WILL NOT WORK!**

I cherish **MY SPOT** in Christ because it's not only unique but also divine. Christ is my refuge, my protection, my intercessor. I am his child. I am a masterpiece of his making. I am a vessel. I'm an instrument of God. I'm an ambassador for Christ. I am his voice in society. Wow! What a great place to be!

I have been sanctified (set aside for the use of God), and I am being molded more into his image daily by every struggle, obstacle, hardship, challenge and disappointment that leads me to victory in Christ. Please remember that God will not allow anything to occur in our lives that does not have a purpose, whether we understand it or not. This gives value and validity to all that happens, good or bad. This means that we have to be willing and submissive in letting go of ego. I was **NEVER** able to accomplish this before intimacy with God.

Though I may not always like the outcome of God's decisions, it gives me courage to endure when I realize that they are not meaningless. This is one of the many divine blessings associated with **MY SPOT.**

This position in Christ affords me a unique intimacy with God. I can commune with him in ways that I have never been able before. I understand things as I have never understood. As a child of God I have a purpose that I never envisioned in the past. Though it is mysterious to some respect, it is perfectly clear that I no longer live a life governed by chance but instead, by the purposes and divine will of God. Therefore, every circumstance has a divine foundation. This gives my life stability and solidarity. I can clearly and confidently embrace the word of God below.

A S A P u b l i s h i n g C o r p o r a t i o n

Romans 8:28-30 (TLB) [28] And we know that all that happens to us is working for our good if we love God and are fitting into his plans.

[29] For from the very beginning God decided that those who came to him—and all along he knew who would—should become like his Son, so that his Son would be the First, with many brothers. [30] And having chosen us, he called us to come to him; and when we came, he declared us "not guilty," filled us with Christ's goodness, gave us right standing with himself, and promised us his glory.

This is not a guarantee that everything will work out well for me or you in this life. Many of God's people suffer gross atrocities worldwide. It means that the purposes of God will be fulfilled, and everything that he has prepared for us will be accomplished.

Therefore, since my position is ordained by God, so are the end results and all the challenges that stood before me in my journey. Though God has allowed me the privilege to bask in this spot, the spot does not belong to me. I am here because of him. Because of this, I must be here for him. I do not own this spot, I am just blessed to reside in it.

Imagine residing in a divine position that

you do not qualify for based on ability or worth, yet you reap all the benefits of the position, as if you earned it, albeit you didn't. What a place to be! What a joy to encounter! What a way to live!

This spot of redemption in which we dwell belongs to God because he provided for all the benefits that abide within it by offering his son Jesus to die on the cross for all of our transgressions. He is the author of our redemption, and being eternal, he is the finisher as well. We, as children of God, are a part of an eternal plan that cannot be altered by time or space. We need not worry about the final analysis. God is in complete control of our eternal destiny.

MY SPOT was secured by the innocent, who was *Jesus,* that the guilty, who was *Me,* could live. We often wonder why the innocent must suffer. However, if we take a closer look at the fatal results of Adam's sin, it will help us in our understanding.

Adam willfully disobeyed God after receiving explicit instructions from him. Unlike Eve, he was *not deceived* by the smooth trickery and the *"play on words"* of Satan. Though I'm certain Adam did not understand the magnitude of his act, he was well aware that he was being disobedient to God, who had warned him prior to Eve being created (Genesis 2:16-17) **NOT** to eat of the tree of the knowledge of good and evil (KJV) yet chose to side with the woman he loved.

Based upon Adam's disobedience, both he and Eve were separated from God in immediate spiritual death, and fell victim to physical death. Though it was not immediate, it was now inevitable. Though physical death was not excluded from those yet to be born, God's grace prevailed over man's spiritual dilemma. To do this, however, the innocent had to die.

Genesis 3:21 (TLB) and the Lord God clothed Adam and his wife with garments made from skins of animals.

Where did these skins come from? Glad you asked! They came from an innocent animal, a symbol, or type, of Christ Jesus, who is our covering. Notice that he clothed them with tunics of **"skin,"** and the one sacrifice clothed them both. The word clothed speaks of blood atonement.

An innocent animal that had nothing to do with Adam's sinful decision was sacrificed for the redemption of the guilty. Jesus, who had nothing to do with Adam's sinful decision, was sacrificed for the redemption of the guilty, which is all humanity. It's important to understand how dreadful a decision Adam made, and it will always result in the innocent suffering.

It's only through the grace of God that we have any worthwhile standing at all. We are NOT the innocent party here. Jesus is the innocent one. This is not about an unfair scenario of the good suffering. Rather, it is a case of sinful people being forgiven by a loving God. This is why I emphasize that, although this is my privileged spot, it is not my space. God owns it. I just graciously occupy it.

Though we are privileged to reside here in this spot, we have no divine authority within it. That authority belongs to God. However, he has given us authority over outside forces that attempt to overthrow us. At the very least, these forces strive to negatively confuse us as to God's purpose. We can, and should, rise up against the outside powers of evil who have pledged enmity toward God and the desire to weaken the solidarity that God has established with us through the blood of Jesus. This is our spot based on God's love toward us. It is his space based on his sovereignty. God is the creator of all things that are good and holy. He is the one who is in total control.

This marvelous position, **MY SPOT,** is secured by the blessed blood of Jesus. It is my responsibility to live in it to the glory of God. When I said **"Yes"** to Jesus, I said **"No"** to society. I said yes to God's way and no to my own. I said yes to God's purposes and no to mine. I said yes to God's methods and no to others.

As tough as this challenge may be at times, it is still our responsibility to strive toward its success because of the marvelous reward of eternal life that is promised to us by God. God's plan for us is greater than the philosophies and ideals of the world. This spot, our position in Christ, requires us to trust God, not with a blind faith that many of our critics accuse us of, but based upon a documented history of life that we are made aware of through the Word of God and validated by our Lord and Savior, Jesus Christ, who constantly quoted the Holy Writ and witnessed to its authenticity. We have documented proof that God is real and is a **"keeper"** of his Word.

This divine position that we find ourselves, as children of God, is secured in the sovereignty, love, faithfulness, and history of Jehovah God. He has not changed in his essence, power, or promises. When you give your life to God through Jesus Christ, you have, without question, made the most important and rewarding decision you will ever make.

Living in the will and testament of God is the safest place in which to dwell. Jesus boldly claimed to not only be the anointed Messiah, but he also had the audacity to claim to be God, which no other had dared claim. It is this truth that the believer stands upon without wavering because of the proof we have in the Word of God. "**WOW!**"

Just because we walk by faith does not mean we stand on an invisible faith. Though we believe in many things we cannot see immediately, our faith is not the result of some "**hocus-pocus theology**" that requires us to believe anything just to believe in something. It is rooted in Jesus Christ, the many witnesses of his earthly ministry, his redemptive suffering and ultimate death on the cross that left us proof that Jehovah is the True and Living God. There are just too many facts, too many witnesses, too many miracles to simply discount the Word of God as folly. Those who choose not to believe in the Word of God have that right; however, that does not "**make**" them right.

I thank God for **MY SPOT**. I don't deserve it, but I will bask in it because grace is defined by its favor to the unworthy. God does not desire our worthiness, only our faithfulness. What a wonderful place to be. Halleluiah for **MY SPOT!**

ASA Publishing Corporation

Chapter 2
Defending MY SPOT

Why do many Christians endure painstaking efforts to defend and protect material things but put so little effort into defending their faith? The answer is painfully simple. **"IT'S NOT VALUABLE ENOUGH!"** It's also because they live in the **"Now"** and not the **"Hereafter."** Many will argue against this. In fact, most will be insulted by such an accusation. However, it is what it is!

I read a quote by Maya Angelo that really captured my attention during a day of reading and relaxation...

> *"Somehow, we have come to the erroneous belief that we are all but flesh, blood, and bones, and that's all. So we direct our values to material things."*

A S A P u b l i s h i n g C o r p o r a t i o n

That **"somehow"** is orchestrated by Satan. He has convinced society, as a whole, that it's all about **"stuff."** It's all about the material things we acquire and how much we accumulate that gives us validation. However, if this is the cure-all, why do we need them over and over again?

1st Peter 3:13-16 (TLB) Usually no one will hurt you for wanting to do good. [14] But even if they should, you are to be envied, for God will reward you for it. [15] Quietly trust yourself to Christ your Lord, and if anybody asks why you believe as you do, be ready to tell him, and do it in a gentle and respectful way.

The English word "apology" comes from a Greek word which basically means "to give a defense." Christian Apologetics, then, is the science of giving a defense of the Christian faith. There are many skeptics who doubt the existence of God and/or attack belief in the God of the Bible. There are many critics who attack the inspiration and infallibility of the Bible. There are many false teachers who promote false doctrines and deny the basic truths of the Christian faith. The mission of Christian Apologetics is to combat these movements and to promote the God of the Bible and the

Christian faith.

I like to call that "Defending **MY SPOT**," that is, having the ability to defend (explain) my belief and conviction in my privileged position in Christ as a child of God as depicted by the Word of God.

Christian Apologetics in its simplest form is presenting a reasonable defense of the Christian faith and truth to those who disagree. Christian Apologetics is a necessary aspect of the Christian life. We are all commanded to be ready and equipped to proclaim the gospel and defend our **faith.** (Matthew 28:18-20; 1 Peter 3:15)

It clearly weakens our ability to influence others if the only explanation we have for people is, *"You need to go to church."* There is more to it than that, and we need to be equipped to defend ourselves. This is where Christian Apologetics can be of great benefit to us.

Every Christian should know what he believes, why he believes it, how to share it with others, and how to defend it against lies and heretical attacks. Though you don't have to be an expert, a preacher, or even an officer in your church, you do have to study the Word of God and become knowledgeable of the Word of God. **YOU HAVE TO STUDY!**

How can we be **"ambassadors of the faith"** if we do not study? Why would we stand on something about which we know very little? What is it that makes us so lackadaisical about the Word of God? Why are we satisfied with saying, **"I go to church?"**

Consider this for a moment. How often have you defended your position regarding other things in your life that you consider important? You find yourself fully prepared to defend your position with valid explanations, facts, statistics, and, if necessary, other witnesses who can validate your claims. Let's look at some simple things that come to my mind that we seem to be readily able to defend. I'm sure you could add many more.

- Your favorite sports team
- Your favorite politician
- Your favorite T.V. program
- Your favorite color
- Your favorite designer
- Your favorite recording artist
- Your favorite teacher

- Your favorite preacher
- Your favorite car
- Your favorite perfume
- Your favorite dance step

How many times have you argued vehemently, and I might add, quite convincingly a particular position you had taken and won over your detractors because of your enthusiasm, passion, conviction and expertise? Are you equipped to do the same when you are confronted by your adversaries regarding your Christian beliefs in God and being saved through the blood of Jesus as your Messiah? WOW! *I hope so!* If not, you may truly need to look at reprioritizing what's important to you.

Have you ever noticed how well prepared the Jehovah's Witnesses, Mormons, and many other cults are when they come knocking on your door or pulling up on their bikes?

Many of you know what I'm talking about, because, at times, I simply didn't answer the door for the Witnesses for fear of being confronted with their expertise, or I'd blow off the kindly bike riders because I was in such a hurry. We know the REAL truth, don't we? The fact is they are very well prepared and knowledgeable of their belief, despite the fact they are actually a cult and not of the True and Living God at all. (Do your own research). Nonetheless, we are the ones who run and hide like varmints. This is primarily due to the fact that we are ill-prepared to defend the very beliefs we claim to embrace. Our churches are filled with people who are filled with spiritual platitudes. We know all the right things to say in church.

Just to name a few:

- Giving honor to God, who is the head of my life.
- God is good all the time, and all the time God is good.
- Let's give God a hand clap of praise.
- Can I get a witness!
- Too blessed to be stressed
- Try our Sundays. They are better than Baskin-Robins.
- Be fishers of men. You catch them. He will clean them.

This is not so much a criticism of these sayings for they are true and for many people quite encouraging. However, my concern is that we have become such gleaners of church phrases and so addicted to the hype of worship service that the Word of God has become an addendum to our worship experience as opposed to the focus. It simply is not held in high esteem, and it should be. What was the Pastor's sermon title the last time you attended church? If you don't know because it wasn't important enough to remember or to write down, then you get my drift.

These phrases may tickle the fancies of many church attenders, but they will not sustain people through life's trials. They certainly will not empower them through Satan's attacks. We make spiritual platitudes the **"meat"** of our existence when they should be the **"witness"** to our experiences. **"God is good,"** we say. If this is true, why don't we desire to know more about him and his purpose for our lives? It's as if God is good as long as he's **DOING** what we want him to do, and not **TELLING** us what to do!

R. C. Sproul, citing 1st Peter 3:15, writes that; *"The defense of the faith is not a luxury or intellectual vanity. It is a task appointed by God that you should be able to give a reason for the hope that is in you as you bear witness before the world."*

We have too much opposition in society to be so casual about our Christian stand. Just settling for being a **"good church member"** is a slap in God's face and a small return for his eternal investment in us. The goodness he has bestowed upon us requires more than that. It involves more than just living a decent life. It's greater than just being a good person.

I have a responsibility to God and my fellow man to be able to defend my position as a child of God. I may not be able to change the world, but I should be willing and quite capable of defending **MY SPOT.** Based on biblical truths, I should be able to clearly explain the necessity of being **"saved."** I should be able to expound on how I got into this sinful mess through the transgression of Adam and further make clear what God did to deliver me from the condemnation of this dreadful act that resulted in my sinful state. This should be done with confidence and with a distinct flavor of academia and expertise.

Disdain and/or the lack of knowledge regarding this sense of responsibility is illustrated by poor attendance at Bible Study in many of our churches, as compared to Sunday morning worship service. Too many Christians feel that church service is enough. It's as if we have no responsibility to promulgate the Word of God. We come on Sundays to get what we can, with no sense of responsibility to learn, grow, and share with others who don't know or understand the truth of the Bible.

I truly believe that this lack of interest and the magnitude of our ignorance regarding the Holy Writ are in direct correlation to Satan's attack upon society as is so clearly stated by the Word of God. We must become more astute about God's Word. It is our responsibility as **"Disciples of Christ."**

Christian Apologetics is the Art and Science of Christian persuasion. There are skills that are required, and they can be obtained if one desires to be better equipped to defend the Word of God. There are classes being offered in your spiritual community if you will seek them. It would be to your advantage to search for seminars or even take a class at a local Bible college just to enrich your knowledge. Invest in your spiritual growth.

Some interesting articles that I read years ago and found during my current research stated that Christians are often some of the worst stewards of any type of education, be it secular or spiritual, because we think God is obligated to do everything for us that we find uncomfortable. I'm often amazed by this pseudo-helplessness when we face discomforting challenges.

When Jesus went to the tomb of Lazarus to raise him from the dead, he did not ask any of the people to assist him in that portion of the miracle. They were incapable of doing so. It is interesting, however, that he required them to move the stone that they had placed over the grave. It was as if he was saying, you put it there, so you move it. Some hindrances that WE have placed in our lives remain there because God is waiting for us to act upon them before he conducts the miraculous part.

For many reasons of their own, Christians have ceased being trail-blazers and have simply become blazer-wearing robots who think that offering God one worship experience a week is indicative of a faithful belief in the grand scheme of God. Wow, how dreadful!

We must pray for and develop, through an involved experience, a greater love and sense of responsibility for studying the Word of God.

We must not shy away from others, rather, we should embrace the opportunity and the need to converse and enlighten them on the soundness of the truth in the Word of God as compared to the theories of man. We must educate ourselves in the spiritual areas we claim to embrace. We must defend our spot. We need to have lay apologists in politics, media, films, journalism, law, medicine, academics, sports, and any other area of life who can help the lost man see his stumbling ways.

I'm afraid that too many of us, as Christians, are so engrossed in ourselves that we are often unaware of our own incompetence. If you can honestly agree that your reasons, or better still, your excuses for being incompetent in the Word of God are not legitimate, then they are ungodly reasons. Unfortunately, there are a lot of people who are that bodacious! The problem with that stance is that, **"IT IS OF THE DEVIL!"** It's another subtle ploy of the devil influencing our thinking.

If you have not taken your Bible Study time seriously, now is the time. Our society is dying from lack of knowledge as it pertains to God. Many Christians are too satisfied being stagnated and confused. Do we just sit back like bumps on a log and let Satan have his way with us? Or, do we stand on the faith we claim to possess and fight back? It's time to reclaim what has been divinely ordained for us, but we must recognize that we have a formidable enemy who is constantly working against us.

You can't defend your spot if you don't know how and why you obtained it. Go to Bible Study at your local church, or find a Bible teaching church to attend their Bible Study, and vow to do a better job of defending your spot. Some lost soul needs to know that those who have the truth know how to explain it. You don't have to be a great orator, when you believe the words will come. This will help minimize the amount of people being duped by false teachers and blind leaders. We owe this to God. He has been too good to us to be so cavalier about our spiritual growth and understanding.

Chapter 3

Building on MY SPOT

John Lennon of the Beatles once wrote:

"When I was 5 years old, my mother always told me that happiness was the key to life. When I went to school, they asked me what I wanted to be when I grew up. I wrote down "happy." They told me that I didn't understand the assignment, and I told them they didn't understand life."

Many people believe that happiness is like chasing the wind. It is impossible to grasp. Well, God doesn't see it that way. "Happy," which is the root meaning of the word "blessed," IS something you can BE, but it must be obtained from the right source.

Happiness is not obtained from outside sources. These sources may satisfy you for a while, but believe me, it will only be for a short time. As an astute detective in a crime mystery noted, **"Given the evidence, this had to be an inside job."** Given the evidence of man's failure to be satisfied by way of outside sources, happiness is fleeting when it is built upon such a weak foundation and nurtured through others who are as flawed as we are. It becomes clearer each day that happiness is an inside job.

When your happiness is based upon the divine will of an eternal God and determined by his purposes, it's not only something you can **"be,"** it's also something others would want to experience. It is a wonderful cycle of reciprocation. The more you pour into others, the more God pours into you. That works for me!

This is what I call, "Building on **MY SPOT**." Remember when I said that I possess the spot, but I don't own it? Well, this develops the mindset within me that I am a steward over my Christian experience and the goodness of God; therefore, I am responsible for how I handle his blessings.

Building on my spot is an inside job. It is

orchestrated by God and can therefore stand up to Satan's trickery. Satan cannot destroy my happiness. Don't get me wrong. It's possible for Satan to destroy me physically, but he can only do that with God's permission. He can wreak complete havoc upon me if God allows him to do so, but he cannot destroy my relationship with God. Thus, he cannot destroy the source of my contentment. He cannot control my inner joy.

He can make me cry, scream, and suffer, but he can't destroy the plan God has for me. Because of this, Satan is constantly trying to keep me from building on **MY SPOT**.

By building on **MY SPOT**, I am promoting the idea of progressively learning more about myself and the importance of surrendering to God. We are always comparing ourselves to other people when judging our progressiveness. Maybe it's time to judge ourselves as God sees us as his people.

Building on my position as a child of God is not about my progress as much as it is about my faithfulness. What looks like failure to people can be quite pleasing to God. It's amazing how we let others define us with their words and the way they respond to us, but we don't give God this same privilege. Most of our self-worth is tied up in how others view us. Instead of putting our positon in Christ on top of our circumstances, we do just the opposite piling our circumstances on top of our position in Christ. Worry! Worry! Worry! Worry! Our position in Christ, **MY SPOT**, gets lost in the shuffle of our everyday grind to survive.

My position in Christ, which I inherited through Jesus Christ, is, by design, a position of authority. It expands as I stand for the cause of Christ. **MY SPOT** not only enlarges because of my faith and obedience, but it also becomes more influential because of the manifestation of God in my life.

The authority that we crave so much in society is actually the result of surrendering to God in the Kingdom. It is that element of the Kingdom of God that we find difficult to understand or accept, yet it is a reality that must be embraced if we are to experience it in our everyday living.

Matthew 8: 5-13 (TLB)

5-6 When Jesus arrived in Capernaum, a Roman army captain came and pled with him to come to his home and heal his servant boy who was in bed paralyzed and racked with pain.

[7] "Yes," Jesus said, "I will come and heal him."

[8-9] Then the officer said, "Sir, I am not worthy to have you in my home; and it isn't necessary for you to come.[b] If you will only stand here and say, 'Be healed,' my servant will get well! I know, because I am under the authority of my superior officers and I have authority over my soldiers, and I say to one, 'Go,' and he goes, and to another, 'Come,' and he comes, and to my slave boy, 'Do this or that,' and he does it. And I know you have authority to tell his sickness to go—and it will go!"

[10] Jesus stood there amazed! Turning to the crowd he said, "I haven't seen faith like this in all the land of Israel! [11] And I tell you this, that many Gentiles like this Roman officer, shall come from all over the world and sit down in the Kingdom of Heaven with Abraham, Isaac, and Jacob. [12] And many an Israelite—those for whom the Kingdom was prepared—shall be cast into outer darkness, into the place of weeping and torment."

[13] Then Jesus said to the Roman officer, "Go on home. What you have believed has happened!"

And the boy was healed that same hour!

The Roman soldier clearly understood the relationship between "under authority" and "authority over." Our authority over is only as powerful as the authority we are under. The soldier's authority to demand his soldiers to "come" and "go"" was based solely upon his submission to the authority of the Roman Army as his superior.

Jesus' earthly authority over, was solely based upon the one he was in submission to, which was his father, Jehovah God. This is how it works! You have authority based on the power of the one to which you are submissive. The more you submit to God the more authority you have. This is crucial to understand in overcoming your circumstances in life. It was not about the Roman captain's individual power. In and of himself, he had no authentic authority over other soldiers. His authority was solely based upon his position of submission to the Roman army itself.

You do not effectively fight in your own power in the first place, but, in the power of God himself. Therefore, building on your spot is determined by how much you relinquish yourself to the will of God. It is no wonder that

Jesus said in Matthew 16:24, "If anyone wants to be a follower of mine, let him deny himself and take up his cross and follow "me"." There is no grey area here -- it's pretty clear! You cannot fight **WITH** God's authority unless you are **UNDER** his authority. That is because if you are not under it, you do not have it with which to fight. Know this truth: You cannot persist on doing things your way and expect to be under the divine authority of God. Despite its clarity, this remains a major roadblock in the lives of many Christians.

Building on your spot is all about the tearing down of **"self."** Yes, you are right. What a contradiction! To build, you must tear down. Are you willing to do that? If not, you are fighting a battle you cannot win.

Trusting God means you must relinquish the trust you have built up in yourself over the years and seek direction through the Word of God regarding every aspect of your life. If you know your decisions do not line up with the Word by way of intent, motive, and execution, you must trust God enough to seek an alternative solution that is in line with his purpose and method.

Initially, this may cause you quite a bit of

discomfort. However, the end result will be in your favor, since the favor of God is upon you. The encouraging part is that it is impossible to fail when doing things God's way. It may be the genesis of some difficulties, but God will not leave you alone to deal with the consequences. God will make you **WAIT**, but he will always lift the **WEIGHT** from your shoulders.

Building on **MY SPOT** is a challenge I choose to embrace because I know it is the will of God and pleasing to him. I have experienced the displeasure of doing things my way for many years in my life. In fact, I became quite efficient at futility. I valued intellect over divine purpose, spiritual energy over God's favor, and experience over eternal wisdom. I just felt I was smart enough to figure out the nuances and mysteries of life. What a mistake that proved to be! In fact, it's a ploy of the "**Wicked One**." As I reflect back, I can't help but wonder how I thought I could possibly have a better handle on life and eternity than the creator of life itself, which is the eternal God. Shucks! I was having trouble just being a participant in life, let alone the ruler. **WOW!**

As a Christian, a child of God, I have grown to recognize that I have a responsibility to God to be obedient and that I am a recipient of his unending love and underserved favor. I am but a very tiny cog in the grand scheme of things. To lose sight of this would encourage me to conjure up a false and destructive arrogance that I have no right to possess.

I have nothing within me worthy of his goodness except the indwelling of the Holy Spirit that I am privileged to possess because of the salvation provided only by God. This responsibility to grow or to build on **MY SPOT** is not a burden of servitude but one of love and gratitude to God for ALL that he has done.

Building on **MY SPOT** is a part of my spiritual growth. It protects me from being distracted by the cunningness of false teachers and spiritual predators wishing to dilute or distort the truth of God to the point that it no longer has relevance by appearing foolish and outdated.

Ephesians 4: 11-16 (TLB)

[11] Some of us have been given special ability as apostles; to others he has given the gift of being able to preach well; some have special ability in winning people to Christ, helping them to trust him as their Savior; still others have a gift for caring for God's people as a shepherd does his

sheep, leading and teaching them in the ways of God.

[12] Why is it that he gives us these special abilities to do certain things best? It is that God's people will be equipped to do better work for him, building up the Church, the body of Christ, to a position of strength and maturity; [13] until finally we all believe alike about our salvation and about our Savior, God's Son, and all become full-grown in the Lord—yes, to the point of being filled full with Christ.

[14] Then we will no longer be like children, forever changing our minds about what we believe because someone has told us something different or has cleverly lied to us and made the lie sound like the truth. [15-16] Instead, we will lovingly follow the truth at all times—speaking truly, dealing truly, living truly—and so become more and more in every way like Christ who is the Head of his body, the Church. Under his direction, the whole body is fitted together perfectly, and each part in its own special way helps the other parts, so that the whole body is healthy and growing and full of love.

It's important to understand that God has an immediate and internal plan for his redeemed people. Your life will no longer be without purpose once you turn it over to God. Though God may never use you for great leadership positions, he will use you all the same. You don't have to be famous to be important to God.

When you build on your position in Christ, you instantly have divine authority available to you. How much of that authority you will be allowed to access will be in relation to how much of yourself you are willing to surrender to God. The Bible is like an instrument panel that sits before you with an enormous amount of capabilities. The more you train on that instrument panel the better you are at getting the most out of it. It's the same with the Bible. The more you study it, the more capable you are of extracting the truths within that empower you.

Building anything requires a plan and disciplined execution. Nothing worthwhile is done overnight. You not only have to be willing, you have to be patient and have the ability to solve problems along the way, all the time trusting in your plan, though you may have to make adjustments.

Too many people let the fear of making adjustments discourage them. Some see them as roadblocks while others who overcome them see them for what they really are, "**bumps in the road.**" When you build on your position, you are not only being obedient, you are displaying your trust (faith) in God, knowing that he will not fail you. You build until it's finished, and it's not finished until this life is over. You build when you feel like it, and you build when you don't.

Just as an expert builder of skyscrapers uses different types of materials, such as steel, iron, concrete, glass, plastics, dirt, etc., to construct his creations, God uses different types of methods to construct us, such as education, success, trials, pain, warfare, and sometimes tragedy. **Remember, the Kingdom of God is a "theocracy," not a "democracy."** We don't get to vote on how God does things.

I really wish I was smart enough to shed some light on solving all of your problems, but the truth is, I'm not. However, I am smart enough to know, through the Word of God, that my position in Christ, **MY SPOT**, is a place of refuge where I refuse to let the devil set up residence and keep me from my spiritual potential and my spiritual blessings. What about you?

A S A   P u b l i s h i n g   C o r p o r a t i o n

Chapter 4

Involved in MY SPOT

During one of my word study sessions, I became inquisitive about the difference between being **"involved"** and being **"engaged."** I found an interesting dichotomy that I thought was enlightening as it pertained to our position in Christ.

This particular company had an interesting view regarding the difference between "engagement" and "involvement," as it related to their employees. It read:

An "engaged" employee, they believed, will understand and agree with the aims and objectives of their business. They will come to work feeling motivated and energized, but unfortunately that's about it.

They concluded that the next step, and one that every business should strive towards, is 'involvement." An involved employee will take an active role in the business. They'll implement new initiatives, take ownership of them and actively participate in driving change.

It was determined that "engagement" is the result of a passive acceptance of company values and objectives. It helps increase productivity, but only to a point. However, "Involvement" is the active pursuit of these objectives. An involved employee will help drive the organization forward and add value to their business. In other words, "engagement" gets you in the game; "involvement" gets you to the top of your game.

Whether you agree with this assessment or not is not the primary concern here. What is at stake, however, is the consideration that attending your church on a regular basis is not necessarily enough to experience the intimacy required to trust God explicitly.

This illustration may, at the very least, compel us to consider that the vastness of God cannot be appreciated with only a nonchalant view of his existence and purpose. God desires a relationship that entails reciprocation. It's a giving and receiving relationship. Though God does not need our personal contributions, since he could do it all without us, he does, however, see our love manifested toward him through our desire to willingly contribute to his plan and purposes.

Are you involved in your relationship with God to the point where you are willing to apply the Word of God to your life on a regular basis, to evoke a change in your thinking and views so that you may become a viable asset to the building of his kingdom over the long haul? Or, have you reached the point that you are satisfied with being engaged enough to enjoy your experience with no desire to play a pivotal role in the Kingdom's overall development?

As a young man, I attended church for many years because I thought it was the right thing to do. I had no real desire to develop an intimate relationship with God. I grew up in a godly home, with godly parents. However, I wanted God in my life as it related to getting what I wanted from life, and from God for that matter. **"Ouch!"**

I was engaged, but not involved. I accepted the truths of the Bible until they collided with my objectives. I wanted God in my life, but I wanted him in my life as it benefitted me in procuring **MY** wants and needs. I attended church based on my particular need for God, without consideration for what God wanted from me. I thought I had the option. Truth is, I didn't. It truly affected my intimacy with God in a negative manner.

In other words, I was **AT** the game, but I was not **IN** the game. I enjoyed being a fan, but I had no desire to be a player. I loved the atmosphere, but the rigors of training, preparation and commitment needed to participate in God's work was not high on my priority list. Oh, I did enough that others admired my participation, but I had no true interest in total submission. I didn't want to become involved.

I did not actively pursue the will of God because I was afraid it would conflict with my desires. I saw no real need to study the Word of God because I did not want to feel any sense of responsibility or accountability. I just wanted to come along for the ride and reap the benefits, whatever they might be, of knowing God without a true commitment to him. You get my drift?

As a pastor, I have experienced this quite frequently. Many people want to be known as regular **"church attenders,"** yet they show no noticeable desire to develop intimacy with God. It boils down to how others see them as opposed to how God sees them. It tends to favor them being respected and admired by other people, as if church is merely a tool to catapult us to a degree of respectability that we cannot experience in any other environment, ie; home, job, marriage etc. This may help explain the lack of interest in the majority of "church attenders" to participate in Bible Study and become students of the Word of God.

For too many people, Sunday Worship is all they need, when predicated upon their intent and objectives. If we use the aforementioned definitions, it's clear that involvement requires much more from us than engagement. When intimacy with God is not a priority, it is not difficult to withhold our best efforts from him. Intimacy requires responsibility. It's like **"wet"** to water. You can't have one without the other.

I am of the persuasion that God wants us involved because giving of ourselves is a direct reflection of God's attribute of love. Giving is a major part of loving, while loving is the foundation for giving. Where there is one you find the other. Any claim of this type of relationship short of this tandem being present is counterfeit.

John 3:16 (TLB) For God loved the world so much that he gave his only Son so that anyone who believes in him shall not perish but have eternal life.

The two key words in this scripture are **"loved"** and **"gave."** They go together like hand and glove. Where there is no desire to give, there is no intent to love. You simply cannot love without giving. It is a natural outpouring of genuine love.

Love is about what you do, as opposed to what you say. I love the saying, **"I'm too busy listening to what you do, to hear what you say."** Action speaks louder than words. Our love for God must be manifested in our actions. It's the only way to reach the **"lost."**

I think it's more important to **"show"** the love of God to the world than to quote scripture that they do not understand. It's better to get involved in others' pain than to define it. People don't care how much you know until they know how much you care.

Getting involved in God's work requires

us to make hardcore decisions. It mandates that we make painful priority decisions.

This is a short excerpt from a speech by David Foster Wallace:

*"There are these two young fish swimming along, and they happen to meet an older fish swimming the other way, who nods at them and says, "Morning, boys, how's the water?" And the two young fish swim on for a bit, and then eventually one of them looks over at the other and goes, "**What is water?**"*

The immediate point of the fish story is that the most obvious and important realities are often the ones that are the hardest to see and talk about. We are often so distracted by the **"art of survival"** that we fail to see the obvious. Man has proven that living without God as the sovereign one leads to the futility of self-gratification based on our own definitions of right and wrong.

This creates the problem of right and wrong being defined by each individual based on their own perception. It promotes the desire to do your own thing and ignore the purposes of God.

The sad thing is, the solution to our

problems is obvious. It is to trust God and not ourselves. Despite the solution being obvious and right at our disposal, we ignore the obvious and swim on, like the two fish, totally oblivious to this important reality.

It's time to get involved in the work of the Lord. Tis time to recognize the futility of our efforts and to pursue the righteousness that will free us from the bondage of engagement, which substitutes activity for results. Just because you are busy does not mean you are effective.

It is crucial that we, as God's people, become involved in Kingdom work. Use the energy, resources and creativity that God has given us to facilitate his work and not ours. This begins with knowledge of the Word of God and ends with a total commitment to his purposes, realizing that the blessings of God will take us further than our most formidable ideas.

- Study The Word Of God
- Pray For Guidance
- Offer Yourselves Individually
- Reach Out To Others
- Support Generously With Your Finances
- Reach Out To The Underprivileged

Kingdom work requires people to get involved and not just engaged. God did not simply engage himself with mankind. He got totally involved. He did not merely recognize that there was a problem, he got involved and solved it. What about you? Are you merely engaged or involved?

Chapter 5

How Faith Works in **MY SPOT**

Hebrews 11:1 (TLB) What is faith? It is the confident assurance that something we want is going to happen. It is the certainty that what we hope for is waiting for us, even though we cannot see it up ahead.

If you looked up the definition of the English word **"faith"** in Webster's Dictionary, and compared it with the Greek word **"pistis"** which is the origin of the word **"faith"** in Hebrews 11:1, it might surprise you that they are very closely related in terms of their meaning.

If you research the two definitions of faith, secular and biblical, you will find a lot of similarities between the two. This is why faith is powerful in both. You don't have to be a child of God to profit from the benefits of the power of faith.

The great inventors and innovators of the past and present were and are the benefactors of the power of their faith. It is their extreme trust and confidence in their dreams and goals that they refused to give up on their inventions and mind boggling innovations that continue to change the world.

However, if you look closely enough, you began to see subtle yet very important differences. Both definitions require confidence, trust, faithfulness and loyalty that foster a dogmatic determination that cannot be extinguished. The significant difference is not the characteristics of faith. Instead, it is the object of the faith.

The issue is not that societal faith and biblical faith have extremely different meanings. They have two different objectives. One faith focuses on trusting people and one's ability and the other focuses on trusting God and his sovereignty. Each can be extraordinarily rewarding, but only one has an eternal impact, and that's the faith that makes God the focus: the biblical faith.

Thus, we find the primary difference.

Now that I am in Christ, faith works entirely different for me in **MY SPOT**. It's not that faith changes from being trust, but the object of my faith has changed. Faith is, totally trusting someone or something to the point of putting all of your confidence in it.

This faith, confidence, and trust that promotes that same determination to achieve in society, must now impact my determination to follow Christ as my Lord and Savior regardless of the obstacles, circumstances and criticisms that I may incur because of my decision.

When other people doubted the dreams of the great inventors and innovators, they forged ahead and never wavered in their faith because they solely believed in their endeavor. They may have been discouraged along the way to success, but they never lost sight of their objective.

As a child of God, faith works for his divine purpose and, therefore, makes him the object of the faith. It's who we believe in, not what. We believe, not simply because of the reward, but because of the character of the person in whom we believe, which is God. Heaven is just a byproduct of the marvelous person that we follow.

God is so awesome, powerful, wise, loving, caring, and so much more, that even if there were no reward at the end of this journey, he is worth our love, and on top of all that he is, we can still look forward to our heavenly reward.

It's amazing how many things we claim to have faith in. We toss the word **"faith"** around pretty loosely. Let's see. We have faith in:

- Our Cars
- Our Golf Clubs
- Our Relatives
- Our Jump Shot
- Our Ability
- Our Teammates

It's not that having confidence in things and people is a sin in and of itself. You have tried and experienced these things and you have grown confident in depending on them to perform up to the quality they have advertised.

The problem is that you may have put an inordinate amount of confidence in people and things that could fail you because none of them possesses perfection. We often find ourselves overwhelmed with disappointment when people and things let us down.

It is impossible not to draw some conclusions about something or someone you have experienced in your life, no matter how short or long term it's been. You draw certain conclusions based on the amount of time spent and the magnitude of the relationship. That trust is okay as long as you keep it within a limited perspective by understanding that at any time failure could occur.

When the object of your faith, regardless of how much faith you think you possess, is questionable, the ultimate experience of obtaining your goal is also called into question. Your faith is only as valuable as the object of your faith is worthy.

When God is the focus of your faith and not the journey, it helps eliminate any discord between God and you. When things get out of sorts, the circumstances become secondary due to your unequivocal trust in God. Charles Stanley often says, **"Trust God and leave the consequences to him."**

This is very important because life is full of ups and downs, unknowns, and injustices. Faith must maintain a maximum degree of integrity to offset the inevitable disappointments that life **WILL** bring. When God is the focus of your faith, then your faith is full of integrity.

Imagine trusting everything and everybody for something as important as life and eternity. Being that everything and everyone is different, your faith would rise and fall daily depending on who is in charge. **There must be a central focus that has control over the ultimate outcome to make your faith valid, and that person is God, though Jesus Christ.**

Someone said this, and I love it! *"You can have a lot of faith in thin ice and drown, or have a little faith in thick ice and live."* It does not matter what amount of faith you have, if the object of your faith is not worthy of it. How long have you trusted your own judgment despite the horrible track record? How many times have you depended on someone that has a history of failure? That's literally setting yourself up for disappointment.

Despite this fact, we continue dancing to the beat of our emotions instead of reason. For instance, what does it matter to have faith in your car for a trip to Africa because it has been well maintained? Your faith is useless because your car is incapable of helping you fulfill your endeavor.

As a child of God, operating in **MY SPOT**, what good is it to have faith in any person or thing that is incapable of fulfilling my objective? Jesus Christ is the almighty propitiation that makes me right with God, fits me for heaven, and secures my relationship with God. Nothing else!

Of course, if you do not want a relationship with God and everlasting life, but only earthly prosperity, it's probably better to have faith in a lot of sources, in hopes that you might pick one that can help you achieve your goal. My faith, in **MY SPOT**, is solely focused on Jesus, because he is the only one that can make me right with God.

The book of Romans, chapters 1-4 (read it for yourself) informs us that we are saved by faith and not good deeds or religion. It is explicit in its explanation that nothing else can do it. In chapter 5, it tells us that the focus of that faith must be Jesus Christ. It does not matter how much faith you have in anything else. Only your belief in Jesus Christ as the Messiah, and the one who died for your redemption will make you right in the sight of God. Notice I said **"right,"** not **"perfect."**

As for me and my house, we will serve the Lord. I love my position in Christ. It's **MY SPOT!**

It's **MY SPOT**:

- ✞ To learn
- ✞ To Grow
- ✞ To Serve
- ✞ To Love
- ✞ To Forgive
- ✞ To Lead

It is such a wonderful and comforting existence to know that my faith is centered around the one who can make a difference. Though there are some wonderful people in my life who have proven themselves to be honest, loving, and trustworthy, my ultimate faith is in God, through Jesus Christ. The best of people often come up short of expectations, myself included. But God never fails. Who else deserves your faith more than he?

Remember your problem may not be a lack of faith at all. All of us have faith in something, even if it's nothing. WOW! Starting today, work at taking all of your trust, confidence, and determination and put them in the hands of the one that can bring you eternal victory. It's no one else except Jesus Christ.

It doesn't matter how long you've had it wrong. Get it right **TODAY!** Yesterday is gone, tomorrow is yet to come, and you only have limited control over today.

Chapter 6

The Ups and Downs of **MY SPOT**

Despite the fact that **MY SPOT** is of divine origin, it is not a perfect spot. God is perfect. We know that. However, the environment in which we experience him is far from it. Our divine existence is acted out in an environment of sin, with animosity toward God all around us. Don't let man's kindness fool you. Man's kindness is not close to God's righteousness.

The Bible tells us that we are in this world but not of it. We must exist within the confines of it, but we must not be controlled by it. Jesus Christ existed in human form in this same environment, but he did not fall victim to it because he was the Son of God and without sin. He never fell short of God's expectations.

However we are not perfect and we fall

A S A P u b l i s h i n g C o r p o r a t i o n

short all the time. Despite this reality, we must never lose our determination to do things God's way. He empowers us to do so through the power of the Holy Spirit. We are indwelled with the capacity to please God in our everyday walk, regardless of our failures.

Though I leave so much to be desired when it comes to pleasing God, I strive daily to repent and rebound from my failures. **It's good to know that since Jesus was nailed to the cross, we are not nailed to my sins**. Forgiveness is just a request away. This assures me that **MY SPOT** is continually of God because of his love for me. This is a part of my new mercies every morning.

So how do we deal with the constant ups and downs of life? First, we must expect them.

Job 14:1-2 (TLB) "How frail is man, how few his days, how full of trouble! ² He blossoms for a moment like a flower—and withers; as the shadow of a passing cloud, he quickly disappears.

The Bible warns us of the rigors and disappointments of life. God never wants us to forget the type of environment in which we live. The world is not getting better, it's getting worse because sin cannot progress in a positive direction. I am not amazed by the digression of mankind, rather at how marvelous God can manifest himself within it.

Every day that tragedy does not strike my household is not a testimony to man's improvement. It's a testimony to God's sovereignty and control over my life. Praise God! **MY SPOT** is not exempt from pain and disappointment. I experience it quite a bit myself. The ups and downs of life frustrate me just as it does others. The difference is, I firmly believe that God has a divine objective for all things. He knows what we don't know and sees what we can't see. Though I may not like the results, I am buoyed by the fact that there is a purpose, and this makes it more tolerable.

I love the knowledge that my problems are not just happenstances that occur. This would leave me empty with no hope of deliverance if no one is in control of my destiny. I want to share this quote:

"When you find your path, you must not be afraid. You need to have sufficient courage to make mistakes. Disappointment, defeat, and despair are the tools God uses to show us the way."
— *Paulo Coelho, Brida*

You ever notice how more attentive we are to God during times of disappointment and failure in our lives? It helps us to understand our vulnerability. It reminds us that we don't have the control we may have thought we had, and there needs to be a dependence on someone greater than us. This may not be a lesson we desire to learn, but it makes us aware of so many things around us to which we had paid no attention.

As I sit and write this book, I am suffering from a slip and fall that fractured my hip. I am now totally dependent on my crutches, which I named **"Fric" and "Frac,"** to get around. It is slow and agonizing. I am limited in my mobility and speed by which I can function. I am so used to go, go, go. Praise God, I am always busy preaching, lecturing and teaching. Therefore, I had questions for God that I wanted answered. Why now, Lord? After 40 years of competitive baseball, football, and basketball, without any major harm, do I experience a significant injury at 66 years old? I could be hindered for months, I thought.

If you know God personally and you communicate on a regular basis, you should know how he responds with the fewest of details at times. It seems when you want one of those in depth and comforting answers to your questions, he appears to be short of words. He simply said, **"Slow down and pay attention to details."** What? I exclaimed!

It's amazing how much I took for granted when I was perfectly able to get around without inhibition or pain. There were a lot of things that I didn't notice. For instance:

❖ There are 14 stairs leading to my second floor
❖ Ice is scary on crutches
❖ Just how vulnerable I really am
❖ There are 11 stairs leading to my basement
❖ There was dust on the baseboards of both sets of stairs
❖ Complaining is the staircase to frustration

Sometimes it takes adversity to slow us down just enough to know how fast we were really going. There are times when we are moving too fast to recognize God's blessings. Sometimes we move at a pace that makes details oblivious to us. Those details are often important to evaluate our situation.

I had a different perspective of David's statement in the 23 Psalm; "Yeah though I <u>walk</u>

through the valley." Of course I would like to **"run"** through my valley experiences. However, this enhances the possibilities of me missing crucial details to which God wants me to personally pay attention. I have learned that valleys in life are not destinations. In fact, they are passageways to greater things. God wants me to appreciate his grace.

How and Why:

- ✓ He kept me from hurt, harm and danger all these years. (it was not my youth)
- ✓ To become more sensitive to the limitations of others
- ✓ Limitations remind us of the necessary vulnerability required to trust God
- ✓ Quickly is not always necessary
- ✓ To adjust to the unknown without losing our zeal to accomplish
- ✓ To put the blessings of God in the right perspective
- ✓ He is the sovereign God of ups and downs
- ✓ We can adjust to any situation if we let God lead us

Of course there were many others I learned, but I chose to mention these.

Pain has a way of making me realize how good God is. The songwriter, Paul Jones, said it this way:

"I've had some good days. I've had some hills to climb. I've had some weary days, and some sleepless nights. But when I look around, and think things over. All of my good days, outweigh my bad days, I won't complain!"

Life is truly an enigma that man cannot solve. I know I can't. We need God to better understand it. There are just too many variables available in life to confuse and bewilder us. But, I serve a God who has everything under control. Life and death is in his hands. Therefore, my destiny is in his hands. How comforting.

During the ups and downs in **MY SPOT**, I have many questions that go unanswered. This is why trusting God is so important.

Of the many things I have grown to understand, this one stands out for me: I am learning to live with unanswered questions. I realize that I don't have to understand all of the **"whys"** of life to enjoy it. God does not owe me an explanation for everything I don't understand. He would have to spend most of his time answering my questions.

I love my position in Christ, **MY SPOT**, but I don't always understand all of the nuances within it. Even as child of God, bad things can happen to good people. If I spent all of my time agonizing over that, I would never get any kingdom work done. I simply rest in his promises. What I have learned is that whatever pain God won't address, he WILL sit with me while I cry. YES! He will never leave me alone.

So many people spend so much time trying to fit God into their lives. This is an endeavor in futility. With all that life demands of us as a husband, wife, employee, mother, father, and friend, how do you find the time to do that? It has nothing to do with your sincerity. It's just impossible to do. It's like trying to get a basketball into a thimble. God is too vast. He's too large and awesome. What we should be doing is placing our lives in God's hands and letting him handle it. It's like placing a marble inside of a barrel. No one should see us, they should only see God. That's how he gets the glory and we get the benefits.

Though **MY SPOT** is not exempt from problems, it is the safest place for me to be because I live within the will of God. Just the thought that I have a friend in Jesus ushers me into the presence of God. He always has my best interest at hand, and that is quite comforting.

He is loving, kind, compassionate, understanding, and faithful. Who would not want a friend such as this?

Remember, this life is all the heaven that a non-believer will ever get. It's no wonder that he strives so hard to experience everything here. What a struggle! On the other hand, this is all the hell a believer will ever see; therefore, hope leaps with joy and expectations. You cannot avoid hardships, but you can overcome them. This is how it is in **MY SPOT**.

Chapter 7

When There Is No Song to Sing in
MY SPOT

Psalms 137: 1-6 (TLB) Weeping, we sat beside the rivers of Babylon thinking of Jerusalem. [2] We have put away our lyres, hanging them upon the branches of the willow trees, [3-4] for how can we sing? Yet our captors, our tormentors, demand that we sing for them the happy songs of Zion! [5-6] If I forget you, O Jerusalem, let my right hand forget its skill upon the harp. If I fail to love her more than my highest joy, let me never sing again.

Earlier we talked about the grind of the ups and downs of life ... you know ... those nuances of life that just can't be avoided because, **"THAT'S LIFE."** However, what about those dark times in your spot when you doubt that you are even in the presence of God, or worse, when you think God doesn't care at all? Ever had those riveting hours of life where there seems very little reason to be happy or thankful? You just couldn't find a song to sing to celebrate your relationship with God. We've all had those dark hours of distrust and disillusionment that we'd rather keep to ourselves.

I don't find many Christians who are willing to admit to these types of days, as if somehow being mad at God is the unforgivable sin. However, I can tell you that I have had some of those days during my Christian journey.

Despite all I know about God and his goodness, there have been times I have found myself completely overwhelmed by the darkness of my circumstances. Some of the real tensions between humans and God are not always pretty, and we shouldn't act as though they don't exist. This reality is worth discussion.

Psalm 137 reflects a time in Israel's (God's chosen people) history when things were so dreadful they could not find a song to sing. Often times the beauty of the Psalms is its disturbing rage resulting from trauma and its honesty as a prayer. Though I have never experienced rage toward God, I have been angry with him on occasion.

The beginning of this psalm records the mourning of God's people in light of their recent captivity to the ungodly nation of Babylon. Their hearts were broken and their spirits trampled by circumstances that didn't show God's favor, which they arrogantly thought they would never lose.

Here they were in a country that did not honor their god. He was of little significance to Babylon, no more than a pebble in a pond. Though the country was pleasant, it offered them no reason to sing. Though they had a history of singing about their god, they struggled to conjure up a song in their present situation.

Whether it resulted from anger, disillusionment, fear, or just their imagination, there was no song to sing, for they were no longer in Jerusalem when they reflected on the glorious temple of God in which they praised him. Now that the temple lay in ruins, they concluded they were no longer in God's presence. It was a time when the omnipresence of God was not fully understood. The city, temple, and altar had been destroyed. There was no worship experience. There were no sacrifices. There were no services unto God. There were no songs to sing.

Still, through it all, their allegiance to God was not broken. Despite having an adverse effect upon their emotional state, they trusted upon their need to remember how good things were in Jerusalem. It was important to reflect back on all that had occurred.

Circumstances can rob us of our desire to sing. Yet, when you find yourself in such a debilitating spiritual state that you feel no need to sing, no need to give God praise, don't beat up on yourself.

It is important to learn from the brokenness of others. God's people were angry. They were hurt. They were filled with disillusionment by their dire circumstances. They cried because of their plight. They rebuked their enemies. Their joy had been destroyed because of their disobedience. There was **NO** song to sing. There was no reason to be happy. There was no blessing to celebrate. Yet, their enemies scornfully demanded a song.

Certain songs elicit a certain emotion. There are songs that make us smile, songs that make us reflect, songs that make us cry, and songs that make us try. There is a power in songs that, at times, is inexplicable. It cannot be denied that they can make a huge impact.

The people of God refused to sing because a joyful song would reflect a forgetfulness of their sorrowful situation and the destruction of Jerusalem. It was not the time to sing. It was a time to reflect. It was a time to mourn. It was a time to realize that all was not good. Believe it or not, there are times in our lives when a song of joy is not appropriate. It's just not spiritually pragmatic to make people sing songs of joy when they should realistically recognize their pain and their situation. There ARE times to mourn our futility and failures.

The people of God hung up their lyres. The times past in Jerusalem were not to be forgotten or taken for granted. This was a time for sadness, to be accountable, a time to be sad.

There are times when we should not attempt to sing our way out of adversity. Instead, we must reflect on how we got there and pay attention to the details of our futility. Israel said we will hang up our instruments of music for another time. It is now that we need to take a realistic assessment of ourselves and our relationship with God.

There are times in **MY SPOT** when there is no song to sing and no reason to celebrate. Rather, they are times to sit, think, and evaluate. We must be careful not to misunderstand the seasons of life with inappropriate songs for the season. When you are hurting, you are hurting. Why should God excuse you from accountability?

We must not take lightly the responsibility of our actions. The people of Israel were suffering as a result of their own disobedience and arrogance because of the choices they made. Though there is no harm in looking for the good in trying circumstances, it should not be done while ignoring responsibility for them. This can result in foolish and immature thinking. Sometimes it is the worst in us that we **NEED** to realize. There are times when you need to cry and **NOT** sing.

There have been times when I tried to sing my way to joy when there was no joy in **MY SPOT**. What I really needed was to recognize the responsibility of my actions. I selfishly used the song of joy to drown out the lyrics of personal failure. It was not to my advantage to sing. Instead, I needed to reflect. I needed to pay attention to what God was teaching and showing me, about me. I didn't need to sing. I needed to cry, to hurt. I needed to appreciate where I was before the pain. I needed to praise God through my growth and understanding, not a song.

Israel's objective was to remember Zion. They were to remember Jerusalem and their privilege to serve God at their highest point. Despite circumstances, they were not to forget their reasons to praise, albeit, not through a song, but through their growth. They deserved to me punished for their disobedience, and they needed to understand why.

We often try to endure the adversities in life without close consideration as to **"WHY"** they may have occurred. Though not **ALL** personal suffering is directly associated with being disobedient to God, many times it is. This requires us to reflect upon the situation to determine if that is the case. We must strive to conclude whether our suffering is for the righteous cause of Christ, or is it the repercussions of ill-fated decisions as a result of doing things our way. If it is the latter, then there is no reason to sing. There is more reason to reflect and resolve.

No matter what situation I may find myself in, there is always a reason to be grateful to God. It could always, and I do mean **ALWAYS**, get worse. Sometimes the fact that I cannot sing leaves me no other alternative than to take a close look at myself to see if I am doing things God's way.

When there is no song to sing in **MY SPOT** and my soul is heavy with regret and sorrow, I find myself very open to the voice of God. His gentle tugging of my thoughts, spirit, and disposition is more comforting than a cool glass of water on a summer day. It doesn't go unnoticed. In my times of sorrow and discomfort, I am learning to reflect back on better times and recognize my privileged position in the lord.

When you can't find a reason to sing, don't give up. Give in to the loving promptings of God, which will sustain you, until you find yourself on the other side of your sorrow. God bless you!

Chapter 8

MY SPOT Is Still Here

Romans 5: 6-10 (TLB) When we were utterly helpless, with no way of escape, Christ came at just the right time and died for us sinners who had no use for him. [7] Even if we were good, we really wouldn't expect anyone to die for us, though, of course, that might be barely possible. But God showed his great love for us by sending Christ to die for us while we were still sinners. [9] And since by his blood he did all this for us as sinners, how much more will he do for us now that he has declared us not guilty? Now he will save us from all of God's wrath to come. [10] And since, when we were his enemies, we were brought back to God by the death of his Son, what blessings he must have for us now that we are his friends and he is living within us!

There is a truth that I can't ignore. That

truth is I have less control over my life than I sometimes claim. Certainly if I had more control, as my subtle arrogance suggests, I would have less sorrow and disappointment in my life. There would seldom be any falling short of my goals and expectations, and a rare need for tears and heartaches. However, there is an evil being named Satan that hates God and therefore, me, and he is always on the attack to destroy the joy I am entitled to in **MY SPOT.**

Every chance Satan gets he tries to move me from **MY SPOT** as often as he can. What I mean by this is that Satan wants me to doubt the promises of God. He wants to compromise my faith in order to influence me and convince me to depend solely on my own ability to perform. This is not to suggest that I become lazy and fail to use the resources that God has given to me. It would, however, never be without God leading and guiding me.

If Satan can convince me to doubt God, he can cunningly convince me to distrust him too. Satan is always attempting to drive a wedge between me and God by challenging God's love for me in times of despair. If God really loved me, Satan suggests, he would not have allowed this adversity to occur. Just as Satan tempted Jesus in the desert, he desires me to worship him and to be showered with my heart's desires. However, I remind myself that God shows the worst first, which is the troubles of this life, and the best last, which is eternal bliss with him. Satan, however, shows the best first, which is whatever you can get in this life, and the worst last, which is eternal damnation.

Remember, Satan has a myriad of methods by which he will attempt to elicit doubt in your mind as it pertains to God's faithfulness. These methods are what I like to call **"spot removers."** It's like coming back to the old neighborhood after being away for years and finding that your favorite playground has been turned into a high rise. He wants you to believe that your position in Christ has been compromised, if not totally alleviated, in order to make you feel helpless. He wants you to give up on God.

Here are some of those methods I'd like to mention. I'm sure you can add to this list.

- o Loss of a loved one
- o Troubled marriage
- o Financial Problems
- o Broken dreams
- o Sickness

- o Rebellious children
- o Broken heart
- o Addictions
- o Unfulfilled life

These are the types of things that will make you wonder if God really cares. These are some of the spot removers in life. They make you forget your privileged position in Christ. They cause you bewilderment and anger toward God and affect your desire to be faithful to him. You can often feel abandoned and stupid for believing in the first place.

The above mentioned hardships are not to be considered only as anomalies of life. They can often be a part of the dark sides of life itself. These circumstances are capable of crumbling the very foundation of our faith. Except for the grace of God, we would be bombarded with these **"Spiritual Missiles"** of mass destruction at any time. These are not reasons to turn **FROM** God. They're reasons to remind us of the necessity to turn **TO** him.

Often, it is because of our mistaken sense of entitlement that we feel no adversity should ever come our way. Sadly, too many of us treat God as if he is the genie in the bottle. We want to use him to fulfill our wishes until we need him again. When God does not fulfill our desires, Satan uses it as a spot remover to convince you that your position in Christ, **MY SPOT**, has been forfeited. The devil has a storehouse of spot removers. Anything available to him that he can use to make you believe your spot has disappeared is fair game. But praise God, I proclaim **MY SPOT** is still here!

The validity of **MY SPOT** has never and never will be determined by my circumstances. Better still, it will never be determined by my performance. It has always been and will always be determined by God's love for me and his grace shown to me.

Romans 5th Chapter informs me that when I was at my worst spiritual state, a sinner, Christ died for me and provided a way for me to be made right with God. Through his propitiation, God's love for me was manifested in the most magnificent way. If God did that for me when I was his enemy, how much more should I expect as his child? Think about it?

Would you give up your life for someone who hates you? Well, that's what God did for the people of God. Though we must not take God's grace for granted by living our lives in any type of manner, how wonderful is it that we don't have to feel like we are walking on egg shells either. God acknowledges our shortcomings, forgives us upon repentance, and renews our fellowship with him. Praise God!

The book of Romans clearly proclaims that God's salvation plan was his ultimate display of love. That kind of love does not dissipate because of the hardships in life or the mistakes we make. God secured my position, **MY SPOT**, with his love and purpose for me.

I am a true believer that my salvation through Jesus Christ cannot be lost through my inability to please God. The truth is I never pleased him in the first place. This is why Jesus had to die for my sins. I was fully condemned at birth. It's not about **"losing"** my salvation, it's all about being a genuine child of God from the beginning. The question is, are you a child of God or just a good church member? There is a distinct difference. You can be a faithful attender of church, and yet, not have an intimate relationship with God.

Satan is constantly attacking my position in Christ, **(MY SPOT)**, through life's circumstances. It's all that he has with which to fight against us. Satan wants me to judge God on what I can see, feel and analyze. If I fall victim to this, I've then relinquished to Satan the most important element of my position, which is faith in God. This makes me vulnerable to believing that **MY SPOT** has been forfeited. The truth is **MY SPOT** is still here, but I must be bold enough, humble enough, and have enough conviction to stand on it.

If you, in fact, buy into the thought that your spot has been forfeited, how then, do you actively participate in the nurturing of your position? How do you gain confidence in what you do in Christ if you don't believe he lives within you by way of the Holy Spirit at all times?

MY SPOT was completely paid for with the precious blood of Jesus. He came to earth as God, dwelling with us in the flesh. When Jesus paid the price for my salvation, he didn't put it in **"lay-away,"** dependent upon future payments. **HE PAID IT IN FULL!** Therefore, there are no more installments necessary. I am in full possession of my position. It is, however, my responsibility to live within it. I have claimed **MY SPOT** because it's rightfully mine.

There must come a time when we, as God's people, must take a stand for what we proclaim to believe. Our belief is only as authentic as the actions that accompany it. We have the propensity to act out that which we believe, whether it's right or wrong. It is our **Actions** that speak the loudest, not our **Words**.

We must be confident that the work God is performing within us will be completed despite the negative impact our humanness may play in its culmination. We are not perfect beings, but we must be sincerely committed to the promptings of the Holy Spirit because we know that God is working within us.

It's very important to understand that God has not offered us anything that he intends to take back from us. That's not how it works. The offer of salvation is not only legitimate, it's also permanent. There is no question about the legitimacy of the offer, only the authenticity of the acceptance. Have you honestly received Christ as your Lord and Savior? Did you merely get caught up in the hype and excitement of the service you attended, or did you truly realize the futility of trying to get right with God on your own terms. Are you willing to turn your life over to him, or are you just trying to fit him into some part of your life?

Jesus died for us because God loved us so

much, even though no one had any love for him initially. What a God we serve! This sacrifice was not made to trick us. We do not have to wonder about our position in Christ, **MY SPOT**. The guessing game is over. If God did that for us while we were "sinners" (people missing the mark), how much more does he intend to do for us as his children? YESSSSS!

Don't allow the rigors of life to make you doubt your standing in Christ. Life was never designed to be fair or just. Sin took away that possibility. What we can rely upon, however, is that our positon in Christ is safe within the evil confines of this life. Of that we can be assured. We are in the world but not of it. We may be impacted by its injustices, but it is not the finality of it all. We have an eternal hope that keeps hope alive. The Apostle Paul said it best.

2 Corinthians 4:7-9 (TLB) [7] But this precious treasure—this light and power that now shine within us—is held in a perishable container, that is, in our weak bodies. Everyone can see that the glorious power within must be from God and is not our own.

[8] We are pressed on every side by troubles, but not crushed and broken. We are perplexed because we don't know why things happen as

they do, but we don't give up and quit. [9] We are hunted down, but God never abandons us. We get knocked down, but we get up again and keep going.

It is because of my position, **MY SPOT**, that these words have power. It is because of what God did for me in Jesus Christ and what he is doing in me through the power of the Holy Spirit.

We must learn to bask in the safety and assurance of our positon. We must be bold in our stance, faithful in our movements, and assured in our disposition.

I have learned that the circumstances of life are not the only gauges by which I must judge God. I must also continue to look forward at the larger picture. I am but a tool in the hands of the Almighty God, Jehovah, to help others see that he, and he alone, is the **"True and Living God."** For this I am both grateful and humbled. I did not deserve to be in this position, but here I am. And you know what? **MY SPOT** is still here!

Chapter 9

All Around **MY SPOT**

Have you ever been in the presence of one of God's people who always seem to be in a state of peace no matter what they are going through? Has it often bewildered and amazed you? Have you wondered what they possess that you don't? Whatever chaos that seemed to surround them, they stood firmly in their faith and belief in God.

We often give credit to people for their ability, strength, and endurance. I know I did. What a marvelous person, I would think to myself. I found myself almost to a point of envying who they were and looking at myself with doubt and disdain. I looked past the grace of God and saw their ability.

Very little good can come out of this perspective because it causes you to focus on the wrong thing. To show you how futile this can be, consider that you will always find someone better looking, smarter, stronger, and more self-assured than yourself. Imagine how many times you would have to become someone you are not, simply trying to be someone else. There will always be people you can learn from and gain a positive perspective without trying to actually be just like them.

This is what the Bible describes as **"straining gnats, and swallowing camels."** You pay attention to needless details, while you miss the greater dangers. When we compare ourselves to others, it's often regarding such things as pretty eyes, smooth skin, white teeth, beautiful hair, financial success, and youthful appearance. These are merely gnats.

How much do these things really matter if you have missed the camels of integrity, honesty, good health, loving family, and peace of mind? In the Kingdom of God, it's not about individuals, it's about family. This can be a very difficult transition that requires much prayer and preparation.

There is a required growth process involving a change of focus and behavior. Too many Christians try to change the way they act without changing their view. They still focus on the gnats of life and miss the camels. I shudder at how many people worry about things short term and lose sight of the objectives that impact their lives for years.

In my opinion, this is because they focus on themselves and not their position in Christ. This certainly had to have an impact on one the most rudimentary requirements of kingdom living.

Luke 9:23 (TLB) Then (Jesus) he said to all, "Anyone who wants to follow me must put aside his own desires and conveniences and carry his cross with him every day and *keep close to me!*

This involves far more than just denying yourselves of objects or pleasures of life. It's greater than that. It involves you understanding that **YOU** are not important in the Kingdom based on how much you think of yourself. Rather, it's honoring the mandates and examples of Christ. This is a much more difficult task. Jesus requires us to emulate him in all things, which includes the way we think. This is more difficult than sacrificing the wonderful amenities of life. This is a phenomenon that transpires from the inside out and is not affected by outward influences. However, it is never without the influence of the object upon which you are focused.

This of course, can be tremendously difficult when everything around me screams, **ME! ME! ME!** I found that all around **MY SPOT** are opposite influences that constantly rip at my inward objective. How, I ask myself, am I to function effectively in **MY SPOT** when surrounded by influences that are antithetical to my spiritual desires? I realize it's all involved in my focus.

If my focus is impacted by my thoughts, then it's important that my thoughts be in alignment with the correct objective, making my focus consistent with my objective. Otherwise, I am fighting against my own efforts, which is a recipe for spiritual frustration. It is imperative, therefore, to determine if my objective is really in line with God. This can only be done through the Word of God. I must fight vehemently against attempting to line God up with my objectives.

This is the fault for many of us, as Christians, for using church attendance as the primary gauge to determine our love and faithfulness to God as well as our alignment with him. Church attendance is not the cure all for the everyday rigors of life. It is an integral part of the relationship because we can be introduced to Christ by hearing the Gospel of salvation preached in the church, and thus receive Christ as Lord and Savior.

However, following our acceptance of Christ, our church attendance becomes the nurturing and service aspect of the relationship. Because of this new intimate relationship with Christ, we are now to learn about him. We are educated in the ways of Christ through the biblical ministries of the church. It is designed to encourage us to fellowship with each other and be a part of their growth through testimonies and encouragement as a member of this great family. Remember, **WE ARE** the church. It was never a building, but a people.

Despite the fact that all around **MY SPOT** there may often be disarray and chaos, the peace within **MY SPOT** is undeniable. This is attainable because within **MY SPOT** I have clearly distinguished the difference between "COMFORTABLE" and "COMFORT." They are not always one and the same. Comfortable is most always determined by an outside source. Comfort is always determined by a source from within. It is not of our doing. Therefore, we are not void of it when we are not in control of our outer resources. We know that God has a divine plan and a divine result for any chaotic situation in our lives, and we can find comfort in knowing that it will work out for his good, if not ours.

It's no secret that what is around us impacts us. However, it should not control us. This is simply putting things into context. What's important is, though we may not be able to change our current situations, we must be cognizant not to let the situation change us. Though this may be easier said than done, it must never cease to be high on our priority list. This is important because whatever is high on our priority list that pleases God will endow him to empower us to either subdue it quickly or give us the patience and wherewithal to endure it over a long period of time. Believe it or not, both are victories, simply different colors.

I have found that all around **MY SPOT** are enemies galore, different types of **"Goliaths"** with legendary reputations lauding their victories. Here are some of those giants.

- Fear
- Doubt

- Past failures
- Debt
- Secrets
- Criticism
- Jealousy
- Lack of ability

These giants challenge me all the time. But you and I must remember that God has blessed us all to have some victories, no matter how small, from which we can draw confidence. These victories are not to be compared to the victories of others because God has his own individual plan for each of us. They are not given for comparison, but to let us know that we, too, are in contact with God.

We must decide if we intend to be people who make a difference or people who make excuses. Which one are you? More importantly, which one do you intend to be? Despite what may be going on around your spot, it's time now to determine what's going on within it.

If it's God's plan to build something within me because of my positon in him, **MY SPOT**, who am I to work against that or to allow someone else to do so? Why would I work against that? God can do so much with so little, he's capable of doing anything with nothing. We know for sure that God can do more with our lives than we ever did. I am a witness! Just because you don't know what God is going to do does not mean it will not be great. You have to trust him. That's the element in **MY SPOT** that can't be overlooked. Ever!

In my many years of ministry I have had a lot of disappointments, just like you. I have cried. I have pondered if I made the right choice. I have wondered if God was listening to me. I have considered quitting. However, I realized that God is larger than my circumstances, and it was foolish trying to fit him in. It was easier to fit my circumstances into his plan. It's amazing how much God will reward you for simply giving to him what he already knows. This is also an opportunity to test your faith.

I may not always understand what's going on in **MY SPOT**, but I do know who has control over it, and it's not me. We spend so much time competing with God over control of our lives that we spiral out of control. Imagine while you are confidently steering your automobile someone reaches over and tries to gain control. Since you know you have complete control over the vehicle, you are reluctant to let go for fear of risking your safety.

Therefore, the wrestling match is on. You won't let go, and neither will they. The result of this conflict could be catastrophic, often more than not.

When we attempt to wrestle control of our lives away from God, there is a unique difference. He will let go of the steering mechanism and let you have it. God is not so weak that he has to compete with us. He is so in control that he will let you have control and never lose his sovereignty in the grand scheme of things. Now that he let you take control of the outside chaos that is now within, your spot has become overwhelmed with the enemy. You are simply in control ... **OF A MESS!**

How intelligent are we really? When you would rather control a mess, rather than be subservient to God's control and prosper, you have to be on the precipice of **INSANITY!** When I realize that God is more powerful than all of my **"goliaths,"** my control becomes a second thought. **My SPOT** is divinely covered; therefore, it's divinely insured. **MY SPOT** is covered by the blood of Jesus. It can neither be stopped nor blocked, no matter what's going on around it.

Injustices are beyond our control. Life

being fair is a fantasy. Pleasing people is an anomaly. Sometimes you do, most times you don't. Isn't it time to start living with some assurances and not just living life by chance? I heard someone say once that, **"We need to stop trying to beat the odds and change the odds."** WOW! It's time to change the way we see things. This will change the way we approach them. When you change the approach, you change the result. Praise God!

I am so glad that I now look at the world from within my position in Christ, **MY SPOT**, as opposed to looking at **MY SPOT** based on outside circumstances. Oh what a relief it is when you know the Master has control! I may not have deserved this position, but I certainly enjoy living in it. Thank you, Lord, for **MY SPOT**!

Be willing to submit to God and change the way you are living because you can't do it alone. Ask Jesus to come into your life because you are ready to receive him and let him change you. It's time to choose the battles you want to fight and not let your circumstances choose them for you.

You don't have to make any ridiculous promises. All you have to do is genuinely receive

Christ, sit at his feet, and learn his ways. He died on the cross for you, was buried, and raised on the third day with all authority to save you from a life of sinfulness. Make a decision today. **"THEN LET GO AND LET GOD!"**

Chapter 10

I Love MY SPOT!

I truly love my position as a child of God because it is not based upon the excellence of my individual performance.

What? You may proclaim. Doesn't God want me to live a holy and righteous life before him? You are absolutely right. God not only wants me to live a life that is a reflection of his love and grace toward me, he also commands that I do so. He wants me to be obedient to his Word and to reflect his holiness in every aspect of my life. However, it is less about my ability to perform and more about my desire to do so. Because Jesus died for my sins, God's love and grace abounds in **MY SPOT**.

God is constantly forgiving us for our human lack of ability to meet his lofty standards; however, our desire to do so should never wane, and we should never weary in our attempt. The Bible clearly warns us against committing evil merely knowing that God is gracious enough to forgive us if we sincerely seek forgiveness. Sometimes the consequences to that evil results in physical death, though our eternal plight is safe. That being said, it is wonderful knowing that every mistake I make will not be saddled upon my record forever if I seek forgiveness and work to change my ways, because Jesus paid the price for my lack.

Jesus' blood is my propitiation (reconciliation) to commune with God. It is through him and him alone. I am neither worthy nor capable of pleasing God on my own. It was God who solved my problem with his plan of salvation that emanated from his great love for me.

The love of God is mindboggling. It's like nothing you have ever experienced. It is beyond anything you can imagine. Don't let the cares of the world deceive you. God loves you with an incomparable love. It can't be explained any clearer than scripture depicts.

John 3:16 For God loved the world so much that he gave his only Son so that anyone who believes in him shall not perish but have eternal life.

Would you give up your only son to die for someone who didn't love you? I can honestly say that I would not have been willing to do so. Thank goodness God is God and not me. However, God's love for us is not wrapped up in emotions. Rather, it's a part of his nature. It's who he is.

I can personally say that God loved me even when I did not display any appreciable love toward him. He loved me as God would, not as a human being would. He loved me because it's not just who he is, but what he does. Despite my faults, he loves me unconditionally. I personally know that I did not love God as I should have. I was not faithful to him, but he was to me.

1 John 4:7-10

[7] Dear friends, let us practice loving each other, for love comes from God and those who are loving and kind show that they are the children of God, and that they are getting to know him better. [8] But if a person isn't loving and kind, it shows that he doesn't know God—for God is love.

[9] God showed how much he loved us by sending his only Son into this wicked world to bring to us eternal life through his death. [10] In this act we see what real love is: it is not our love for God but his love for us when he sent his Son to satisfy God's anger against our sins.

This type of love should not be taken lightly. Who else do you know that would love you in such a manner? God does not love us because we love him. He loves us because he is love. More the reason we should have a genuine love for him.

I love **MY SPOT** because not only did it originate from love, it also is maintained because of it. God's love for me is not an event. Rather, it is an ongoing reality. It doesn't just happen once and I am then left to my own ability to perform. God empowers me to continue to be pleasing unto him through the power of the Holy Spirit.

I don't know about you, but there are times I must remind myself of this wonderful gift of divine power. I am so thankful for the substitutionary death of our Lord and Savior, Jesus Christ, on the cross, that I sometimes lose sight of the present gift of the Holt Spirit within me.

It is this continuous gift of love from God that I must never take for granted. God has not left me to feign for myself. He has sent me an advocate, an advisor, if you will, to instruct and empower me to do the will of God. It is so comforting to know that I do not have to labor fruitlessly for God's favor. It was granted to me by receiving Christ as my savior.

What I constantly strive for, however, is to live the love I have received from God so that others might see the divine love and graciousness that resides within **MY SPOT**. It is the desire to please God, not my performance that is most important. If my desire is genuine, my performance will take care of itself the more I submit to the Holy Spirit. God cannot fail. This assures me of fulfilling his purpose in my life as I allow him to lead me.

My position in Christ, **MY SPOT**, was never designed for me to gain individual recognition to hoard for myself. If God grants recognition, so be it. However, it is for God to get the glory in my efforts. Certainly, being human, I, like you, must fight daily against the desires to be well known, highly regarded, and deeply appreciated. This is a constant struggle for any of us because we fight against human desires all the time.

Because the Holy Spirit reigns in **MY SPOT**, it helps to keep me in check. It reminds me that all I may be, or may become, is due to God's grace, and not my efforts. The efforts are merely my response to his undying love for me. What God does with my efforts is solely up to him. Actually, this takes so much pressure off me because I'm not the one who is **IN** control, though God may let me sit **AT** the control panel.

Imagine simply having to do things God's way and all of the responsibility for the results are on his shoulders and not yours. I love **MY SPOT** because it is based not only on the promises of God but also on his power and authority to effectuate them. **WOW!** Oh what a relief it is.

Matthew 11:28 (TLB)

[28] Come to me and I will give you rest—all of you who work so hard beneath a heavy yoke. Wear my yoke—for it fits perfectly—and let me teach you; for I am gentle and humble, and you shall find rest for your souls; for I give you

only light burdens."

I shudder to think how many years I labored to get right with God and failed miserably. I dealt with the futility of living up to his standards under my own power, when it was my desire to please that was lacking. Like me, many people declare that they want to please God. However, they want to do it on their terms. They fail to see, as I did, that this is a form of rebellion. If you want to do it **YOUR** way, then you have no desire to do it **HIS** way. You can't have it both ways!

I had to learn to rest in Jesus' yoke and not mine. All of my desire to do things God's way did not always emanate from willing compliance. Some of it resulted from my continuous failure. The truth is, it does not matter **HOW** you get it, just that you do. The **"prodigal son"** had to lose it all before he realized the importance of his father's love. It truly was a burdensome yoke trying to guess my way through life, instead of standing on God's promises.

Have you ever considered how many centuries scripture has been tried and tested? Have you thought of the many people who have been richly rewarded by their faith in God?

Which history has been more authentic, yours or God's? Who is most trustworthy, you or God?

It's really amazing how long it took me to understand this. How could I take the simplicity of God's request to rest in his yoke and turn it into a complex debate based upon my intellect? I could not understand this kind of love. Who creates a plan for rescue and then provides the power do so? Who guarantees your deliverance despite your own inability to execute? No one... except the **"True and Living God,"** Jehovah. I "lovvvvvve" MY SPOT!

MY SPOT is not only based upon the love of God, it is continuously permeated with his love. God loves me on my worst days. He looks past my faults and recognizes my needs. He is constantly reconfiguring my desires through his Word. It is not my actions that determine a rebellious spirit as much as it is my desires.

Have you ever watched one of your children who had the right motive but failed at the attempt to execute a plan? Do you remember how much compassion you had for them? That's what God is looking for in our hearts, the right motive. Do you have a heart to please God? If so, he will reach out to you and empower you to do so. This is not because we deserve it. Rather, it's because of the spot in which you reside. It is wrapped up in his promises and faithfulness to us. God is awesome!

Remember when God promised Israel the land of Canaan? He told them that he would give them a land **"flowing with milk and honey."** However, the catch was someone else was dwelling in the land. Someone else was living there! Why give away land that belonged to someone else, you might think.

Joshua 24:8-15 (TLB)

"'Finally I brought you into the land of the Amorites on the other side of the Jordan; and they fought against you, but I destroyed them and gave you their land. 9 Then King Balak of Moab started a war against Israel, and he asked Balaam, the son of Beor, to curse you. 10 But I wouldn't listen to him. Instead I made him bless you; and so I delivered Israel from him.

11 "'Then you crossed the Jordan River and came to Jericho. The men of Jericho fought against you, and so did many others—the Perizzites, the Canaanites, the Hittites, the Girgashites,

the Hivites, and the Jebusites. Each in turn fought against you, but I destroyed them all. ¹² And I sent hornets ahead of you to drive out the two kings of the Amorites and their people. It was not your swords or bows that brought you victory! ¹³ I gave you land you had not worked for and cities you did not build—these cities where you are now living. I gave you vineyards and olive groves for food, though you did not plant them.'

¹⁴ "So revere Jehovah and serve him in sincerity and truth. Put away forever the idols your ancestors worshiped when they lived beyond the Euphrates River and in Egypt. Worship the Lord alone. ¹⁵ But if you are unwilling to obey the Lord, then decide today whom you will obey. Will it be the gods of your ancestors beyond the Euphrates or the gods of the Amorites here in this land? But as for me and my family, we will serve the Lord."

Well, I truly believe that one of the reasons for this was for them to rest in his promises and let someone else till the land, plant the vineyards, and build the houses. This way all God's people had to do was move in.

There are so many promises God has in store for us, but he will often allow those who resist him and do not honor him to secure the position for us. All we have to do is walk by faith and not by sight to reap the benefits. This is not to imply that life will be a breeze. It is, however, a reminder that every obstacle, struggle, and disappointment is not always an indication of failure, but a divine delay until the project is finished.

It may have taken me a while, but I hope my futility is your blessing. Don't put off another day to receive Christ as your Lord and Savior. Receive him now and watch him work

If you know the Lord in the pardoning of your sins, yet you struggle to give in, trust the Holy Spirit to lead you in the right direction. There is nothing like being **"in Christ."** It is a divine position, with a divine purpose, that will produce a divine result. Man! I love **MY SPOT!**

Thank you for traveling this short journey with me. I hope that in some way I was able to influence you to have a greater appreciation for your position **in Christ Jesus**. There is no better way to live with the complexities of life than to live it under the divine presence and purpose of God.

God bless you!!!

This is MY SPOT
Celebrating My Position In Christ

It's only through the grace of God that we have any worthwhile standing at all. We are NOT the innocent party here. Jesus is the innocent one. This is not about the unfair scenario of the good suffering. Rather, it is a case of sinful people being forgiven by a loving God. This is why I emphasize that, although this is my privileged spot, it is not my space. God owns it. I just graciously occupy it.

Why God?

Imagine trusting everyone and everything for something as important as life and eternity. Being that everyone and everything is different, your faith would rise and fall daily depending on who is in charge. There must be a central focus that has control over the ultimate outcome to make your faith valid, and that person is God, through Jesus Christ.

It is good to know that since Jesus was nailed to the cross, we are not nailed to our sins. Forgiveness is just a request away. This assures me that **"MY SPOT"** is continually of God because of his love for me. This is part of my new mercies every morning, and I pray it's the same for you!

ISBN 978-1-886528-94

5 12

9 781886 528949

ASA Publishing Corporation